Kenya

After the British built a railroad through Kenya in the 1890s, white farmers settled in large numbers, and Indian laborers who came to build the railroad also stayed. Since becoming independent in 1963, Kenya has managed to increase its prosperity by striving to weld the various tribes into a single nation, retaining the loyalty of its settlers, avoiding internal warfare, and living peaceably with its neighbors.

Kenya's economy is still dependent on agriculture, and it is one of the world's largest exporters of tea and coffee. However, its manufacturing sector is expanding rapidly.

Mohamed Amin and Zulf Khalfan are well-known photojournalists living in Nairobi, Kenya's capital. They traveled all over the country to gather these twenty-six accounts of life in Kenya's cities, bushlands, and farms.

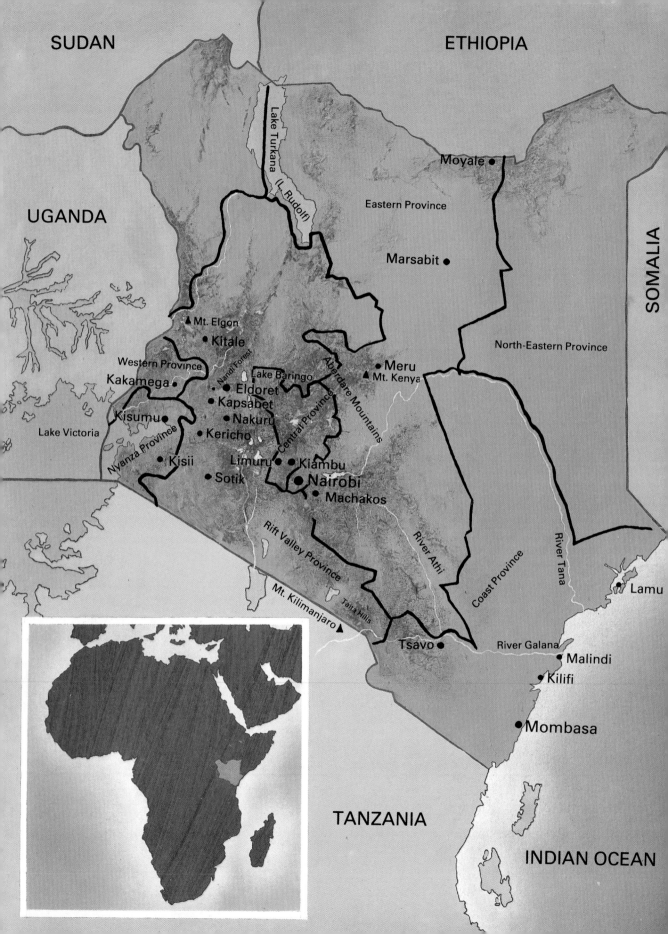

SUDAN

ETHIOPIA

Lake Turkana
(L. Rudolf)

Moyale •

UGANDA

Eastern Province

Marsabit •

SOMALIA

North-Eastern Province

▲ Mt. Elgon

• Kitale

Western Province

Nandi Forest

Lake Baringo

Aberdare Mountains

• Meru

Kakamega •

• Eldoret

▲ Mt. Kenya

Kisumu •

• Kapsabet

• Nakuru

Central Province

Lake Victoria

Nyanza Province

• Kericho

• Kisii

Limuru •

• Kiambu

• Sotik

Nairobi

Machakos

River Athi

River Tana

Rift Valley Province

Coast Province

Lamu •

Mt. Kilimanjaro ▲

Taita Hills

Tsavo •

River Galana

• Malindi

• Kilifi

• Mombasa

TANZANIA

INDIAN OCEAN

we live in
KENYA

Zulf M Khalfan and Mohamed Amin

A Living Here Book
The Bookwright Press
New York · 1984

Living Here

First published in the United States in 1984 by
The Bookwright Press, 387 Park Avenue South,
New York, NY 10016

First published in Great Britain in 1983 by
Wayland (Publishers) Ltd
49 Lansdowne Place, Hove
East Sussex BN3 1HF, England

© Copyright 1983 Wayland (Publishers) Ltd

ISBN 0–531–03797–5
Library of Congress Catalog Card Number: 84–70776

Printed by G. Canale & C.S.p.A., Turin, Italy

Contents

"246 babies die out of every 1,000 born"

Phoebe Asiyo is the MP (Member of Parliament) for the constituency of Karachuonyo, on the eastern shores of Lake Victoria. She is one of the four women currently in Kenya's Parliament. She is striving to improve the status of women in Kenya.

Kenya became independent on December 12, 1963. (Since 1923 Kenya had been a British colony.) A year later, our republican constitution came into being, and it was revised in 1969. The current Head of State is President Daniel arap Moi. He is advised by a Vice-President and a Cabinet, both of whom he appoints from Members of Parliament. There are 26 Ministers in the Cabinet, assisted by 51 Assistant Ministers.

Kenya has a single-chamber Parliament, called the National Assembly. It has 158 elected members (including the President), 12 members nominated by the President, a Speaker (elected by the National Assembly) and an Attorney General (a civil servant appointed by the President). Currently, there are four women MPs (three have been elected, and one was appointed by the President). There is a general election every five years to elect the National Assembly.

I became the MP for Karachuonyo in 1979, defeating four men in the elections!

Being on the shores of Lake Victoria, my constituents are mainly fishermen and farmers. Peanuts and cotton (our cotton yield in 1981 was worth six million shillings) are the main crops around here. Unfortunately, my constituency has the highest infant mortality rate in the whole of Kenya: 246 babies die out of every 1,000 born – that's almost 25 percent. Water-borne diseases and malaria are the main causes of this. The government is trying to improve things by making people more aware of the importance of hygiene and a clean environment.

People have high expectations of an MP. They see us as providers; people who should help to supply them with their basic needs – jobs, food, good health and shelter. I believe in motivating people to help themselves. They must not expect the government to provide them with everything on a plate. I'm encouraging the government to set up more *Harambee* projects. *Harambee* is Kenya's motto. It means "pulling together" or "self-help."

I visit my constituency every week. I have a head office there and twenty-nine "mini offices." I try to visit them all regularly, either to discuss problems with people or to address meetings. But getting around can be a bit of a problem. Some areas of my constituency have poor roads and cannot be reached by car, so I have to use a bicycle – or my feet!

I enjoy meeting people and helping to solve their problems. I was a social worker before entering politics, which prepared me for the work of an MP. As an MP, I'm trying to improve the status of women in Kenya, an issue that has interested me for a long time. In 1959, I was elected the first chairperson of the *Maendeleo ya Wanawake* (Development of Women) organization. I wish more women in Kenya would accept challenges. A woman has to work three times harder than a man to get anywhere. But once you've got to a responsible position, men accept you and appreciate your capabilities. Women must develop the courage and determination to lead, and not be prepared to be second-best to a man.

The interior of Kenya's Parliament in Nairobi.

Two Masai voting at a general election, held every five years. Kenya has 158 MPs.

"There's no railroad line to the north"

Martin Nguli is a train engineer with the Kenyan Railways Corporation. He has been working on the railroads for twenty-three years. He comes from the town of Machakos, in the Eastern Province. He is married with seven children.

I joined Kenyan Railways in the days of the steam engine. It was unbearably hot in them. Now we have diesel locomotives, about 330 of them, which are more comfortable. In 1981, we carried 4,900,000 tons of freight and some 2,300,000 passengers. Our passenger services are divided into first, second and third class. It costs 324 shillings to travel first class from Nairobi to Mombasa, a distance of 485 kilometers (300 miles), which takes 14 hours.

The railroad line from the coast was built by the British at the end of the nineteenth century to give Uganda access to a port. It has been expanded a lot since then but there's no railroad line to the far north because few people live there and it's not very productive agriculturally — it's either desert or semi-arid.

In 1981, Kenyan Railways carried some 2,300,000 passengers. The railroad was built in the 1890s.

It's a wonderful experience to travel from Mombasa right across Kenya to Uganda. You start at sea level and travel through Tsavo National Park and across the Athi Plains, with its teeming wildlife, up to Nairobi. From here, the railroad climbs 900 meters (3,000 feet) as it heads for Limuru, a farming town on the edge of the Great Rift Valley. Then it plunges virtually to the floor of the valley, passing Mount Longonot, a dormant volcano with its yawning crater and bubbling thermal springs at its base, and heads for Naivasha, a popular holiday resort near Lake Naivasha.

Then on past Lake Elementaita to Nakuru, the farming capital of Kenya. You pass Lake Nakuru, a bird-watcher's

An old steam engine pulling freight cars through a remote part of Kenya.

paradise, and cross Nakuru National Park with its fifty kinds of game. Now you climb to the Equator, crossing it at 2,740 meters (9,136 feet) near Timboroa, one of the coldest parts of Kenya. Passing through more fertile farmland, you reach Eldoret, a busy, expanding industrial town and the last major settlement before the Ugandan border. Before you reach it, you go through Webuye, famed for the awful smell from the Pan-African Paper Mills, making paper out of logs twenty-four hours a day! Then the railroad rolls on to Tororo and to the cassava and banana plantations of Uganda.

9

"Old people are full of information"

Athman Lali Omar is the 28-year-old curator of the Lamu Museum. Lamu is a group of islands, with a population of about 8,000, off the coast. Athman lives with his wife in a stone house built in the ninth century A.D.

I'm a rather unusual museum curator because much of my time is taken up in work away from the museum, supervising archaeological excavations and the conservation of many historical monuments and buildings. I'm the only government official in Kenya with a job like this. Most of my work is done in the coastal regions between our border with Somalia and the River Tana's delta. Some of the buildings in this area date back to the ninth century. The oldest ones were built by the Swahilis, the more recent ones by Arabs from the Persian Gulf who used to trade along this coast in early times. I have to make sure that these buildings are not being destroyed by the weather or wildlife, and repair any damage to them.

I stay in the museum during the rainy seasons, because it's very difficult to get around then. We have two rainy seasons in Kenya: the "long" rains between March and May, when it rains heavily for about two and a half months; and the "short" rains between October and November, when it rains for about six weeks.

Being a Swahili has helped a lot in my work. Most of the people around here are Swahilis, so I'm "one of them": they don't

Cannons being excavated at Siyu Fort on Siyu Island, off Lamu. Athman is in charge of the work.

distrust me as they do outsiders. It's difficult for an outsider to penetrate a traditional society like the one we have on Lamu Island. People are reluctant to talk to strangers, but not to me. Whenever we have a problem at the museum – finding an unusual object, for example – we go and talk to one of the old people on the island. They're full of useful information on how life used to be in these parts, and can also remember things that their parents told them. In Africa, much has been passed down from one generation to the next by the spoken word; little has been written down. We have just put on an exhibition on henna, *hina* in Swahili, which women on the coast use a lot. While we were organizing it, we invited some of the old women here and they told us a lot of useful things about the history of henna.

Many people complain that Kenyan museums are only for the tourists, but this one has been set up primarily for the *wananchi* (Kenyan citizens). We've encouraged the local people to become involved in the restoration and conservation of our old buildings and in the setting up of exhibitions. As a result, people around here seem more aware of the cultural value of things that perhaps their grandparents have left them. People have even given us items to display in the museum. This is very gratifying, especially as many rich collectors have been buying Kenyan antiques and then exporting them.

An aerial view of Fort Jesus on Lamu Island, built in the 16th century by the Portuguese.

"Kenya has about forty tribes"

Kibiy Mutai is an elder of the Nandi tribe, who owns twenty cattle. He doesn't know his age, but thinks he is about 60. He lives in a mud-and-grass thatched house near in the Nandi Forest, in the Rift Valley Province.

As an elder, the younger members of my tribe come to me to ask for my opinion on things and for advice on tribal matters. Elders are respected members of the tribe. They are obeyed and sometimes revered. Respect for elders is an age-old African tradition. No, an elder is not employed by the tribe. In appreciation for what he does for his tribe, he may get gifts or tokens, such as a goat, a sheep, a walking stick or a pipe.

Kenya has about forty tribes, some of which are related. The Nandis, for example, are related to the Kipsigis and five other tribes; together we're known as the Kalenjin. The tribes have different ways of life. On the coast and on the lakes, they are fishermen. Up in the north, we have desert people. The Tharaka tribe, who live along the banks of the River Tana, in the east, are honey gatherers.

Kibiy's two-roomed, thatched house in Kaitei.

Here, in the rolling Nandi Hills, we've been blessed with fertile soil, so we're mainly farmers. We grow millet, sorghum, corn, beans, potatoes, tobacco, bananas, and pyrethrum, which is used in insecticides. We also rear sheep and cattle. Our farms are mostly small plots of less than 20 hectares (50 acres), but they are very efficient, like most small farms in Kenya. I've heard that a couple of years ago, small farms in Kenya produced 1.8 million tons of corn, over 800,000 tons of potatoes, about 660,000 tons of beans, and about 488,000 tons of vegetables. The Nandi District itself has about 234,000 hectares (585,000 acres) of high-potential agricultural land.

Cattle are important to us, for their material and spiritual value. A cattle enclosure is an essential part of our homesteads. Twenty of our homesteads form a *koret* (a Nandi parish) and, in the past, about a dozen *korets* made up a *poroiret*. A *poroiret* was governed by a council of elders. The leader of the council was not elected: it was the most wealthy person, because he could entertain others better with food and drink. The council dealt with disputes over cattle or marriage dowries, and decided on compensation for families who had had someone murdered. Nowadays, a handful of elders gather to settle problems.

We believe in *Asis* (God). Nandis may be troubled by *Oiik*, the spirits of our departed ancestors. They bring sickness or death. We see them in our dreams. Milk, beer and some food is offered in a ceremony to appease them. When we have a new moon, we bless the young by spitting on them.

The elders supervise circumcision rites for our young boys; there used to be a similar ceremony for young girls, but it has been banned. Circumcision is done between 10 and 11 years old. The elders take the boys into the forest, where they build huts for the ceremony. After the operation, the boys go into seclusion and are instructed on how to live like good, responsible and courageous adults. Circumcision marks their transition into manhood.

We're proud of the history of our warriors. Nandi warriors fought against British troops in Kenya at the turn of the century. Later, Nandis fought with the British in the First and Second World Wars. Nandis have produced top-rank athletes, too, such as Kipchoge Keino and Henry Rono, a runner who held three world records. We're proud of the honor they've brought to Kenya.

Kibiy with one of his cows. Cattle are important for their spiritual and material value.

"I've been under this tree since 1971!"

Mwangi Njeru Muturi is a 53-year-old herbalist who works under a tree near the Central Bus Station in Nairobi. Married with three children, he lives in a four-room mud house in Kariobangi, Nairobi.

I'm a traditional medicine man – a herbalist. We obtain our herbs from plants and the branches, roots, and barks of trees. We boil these to make medicine. Some of our medicines are powdered and are taken with milk, tea, water, or soup; others are extracted in juice form and taken straight. These tend to be stronger than powdered medicines. They are for serious illnesses: diabetes, for example. I'm not going to tell you the names of the herbs I use. They're a professional secret. I'll talk to a modern doctor about a particular herb and its effects, but that's different – we're both in the same business.

I treat mainly stomach disorders, such as ulcers. People also come to me because they have backache or headaches, but I don't treat eye complaints. You have to be very careful when dealing with eyes.

How do I diagnose my patients? Listen. For generations, before we had medical

Mwangi sets out his medicines on his stall at the start of another day's business.

schools, people used to be treated by our *wazees* (elders). Their healing powers have been passed on to us by our forefathers as a gift from God. My father was a herbalist and I learned a lot from him. I've been a herbalist for twelve years now and I've been kept busy. I've been under this tree since 1971! I don't wait for the medicine to be brought to me. I go out into the bush to look for it!

Once I had a very bad cough, which couldn't be treated. I was very sick, and I couldn't work properly. So I decided to try a medicine shown to me by my grandfather. I asked a friend to find a particular plant and bring me a branch and a root. I boiled these and drank the extract, a few spoonfuls, in a cup of soup. Then I had a long sleep, from the afternoon till the following morning. I took the medicine again two days later. It cured me. Since then I've never had the complaint again. When I fall sick, I go to either a herbalist or a doctor. It depends on what's wrong with me.

It's very important for modern doctors to cooperate with herbalists. We should help each other, instead of keeping apart. After all, we're both doing the same thing – curing people of their illnesses. And the medicines we use are basically the same.

However, one advantage that modern medicine has over us is that it can extract drugs from plants *and* animals. But the drugs it gets from plants are the same as mine. So we should work together. Some modern doctors come to talk to herbalists, but most of them are suspicious and distrustful about our education. They ask such questions as: "What are your qualifications?" Only a few of them understand us. They're the ones who say: "Come over, let's talk."

Bad illnesses are those that have stayed with the patient for a very long time. They defeat even modern doctors. They might defeat me too. It could be a disease which has spread all over the patient's system. Then nothing can be done.

There are many herbalists in Kenya. There are also faith healers, and witch doctors. All kinds of people come to me. Some days up to half a dozen visit me; other days none. Some are scared of me; others look down upon herbalism, thinking: "How does *he* know what's wrong with me?" But those that are treated and get cured come to believe in my powers.

15

"Kenya is a good farming country"

David Powell is the manager of a coffee plantation. He lives in Kiambu, in the heart of Kenya's coffee-growing area. Born in England, he has lived in Kenya for most of his life.

I've been in Kenya since 1939. Life seemed to be easier then. You didn't worry about whether your pockets were full of money or not. Now life is much more difficult. You've got to be careful with your money. Our salaries aren't keeping pace with inflation, now about 20 percent a year.

This plantation, or *shamba* in Swahili, is 84 hectares (208 acres). Of this, 62 hectares (155 acres) are planted with coffee,

After being picked, the coffee beans are dried in the sun on long tables like these.

with some 90,000 Arabica plants.

The coffee is picked twice a year: the early crop around May-June, and the late crop around November-December. The pickers are day laborers, from around this area. They collect the berries in a *debe* (old kerosene can). They get paid three shillings per *debe*. A picker averages about four *debes* daily. The pickers start work at 7:00 a.m. and usually don't stop until 5:00 p.m.

I've been running this *shamba* since 1961. It used to belong to my aunt and she

left it to me when she died. My late wife and I took it over when it was almost bankrupt. It was a struggle to get it back on its feet. In 1976, we sold it to the present owner, a Kenyan African. I've been the manager since then. I think there are quite a few other estates like this, originally owned by Europeans, now sold back to Africans.

We produce about 100 tons of coffee a year, although we once picked 246 tons. We send our coffee to the Kenya Plantation Co-operative Union (KPCU). It arranges the marketing and selling of it through the Coffee Marketing Board (CMB). It's quite a good marketing system.

In 1981, 100,000 tons of coffee were delivered to the CMB. We were paid about K£1,129 per ton. But coffee fetched a much lower price in the world market: in May-June 1981, it was about K£795 per ton. That year, Kenya exported 97,600 tons, worth some K£109.4 million in world markets.

Kenya is a good farming country but the farms seem to be poorly run. Back in the late Thirties, I worked on a European-owned farm. The place was a hive of industry! The owner's wife used to have a vegetable garden of about 6 hectares (15 acres). Her vegetables and fruits were sent all over East Africa – to Nairobi, Kampala, and Dar-es-Salaam – twice a week. They had everything on that farm – cattle, sheep, pigs, pyrethrum, and cereals. Everything was go go go! It was very productive, as were the other farms. Two years ago, I went back to the farm to look around. I wasn't that impressed with what was going on.

Most of the large farms have now been cut up into small plots, which can only produce enough for their owners to live on: little is left over to sell.

David checks that a seasonal coffee-picker is doing her job properly. The coffee is picked twice a year.

There are nearly 40,000 Europeans in Kenya. Many have emigrated here; others have come to work for the government or for the large corporations which have big investments in Kenya.

A lot of people come here from Nairobi, because the climate is milder. We're 1,800 meters (5,700 feet) above sea level, higher than Nairobi. I'd rather not live anywhere else. No, I don't want to go back to England. Never! I was last there in 1973, and found it claustrophobic.

"Women are not considered newsworthy!"

Eunice Njambi Mathu lives in a suburb of Nairobi, and is the owner and editor of *Consumer's Digest*. She is also Chairperson of the Association of Media Women in Kenya.

We have five daily newspapers – the *Standard*, the *Nation*, the *Kenya Times*, the *Taifaleo*, and *Kenya Leo*. The first three are in English and the last two in Swahili. The *Nation* has the largest circulation, selling about 110,000 copies; the other four sell about 54,000 each. In addition, we have five weekly newspapers: four in English and one in German, English and Swahili; of these, the *Sunday Nation* has the largest

Eunice with her husband and two young sons in the garden of her home in a suburb of Nairobi.

circulation (115,000 copies), followed by the *Sunday Standard* (46,000 copies). We also have a variety of trade, technical and sports magazines.

Of all the mass-communications media in Kenya, radio is by far the most important and effective. This is because we have a fairly low level of literacy. Recent surveys show that only 48 percent of the population in rural areas is literate; although in the Central Province (where Nairobi is), the level rises to 60 percent. Our radio broadcasting system is one of the oldest in Africa. It's been operating for fifty years.

The Voice of Kenya (VOK) is run by the government and has three services: the General Service in English; the National Service in Swahili; and the Vernacular Service in sixteen languages. VOK broadcasts to schools and also has radio correspondence courses on such things as farming. There are about 1.5 million radio sets in Kenya, and it has been estimated that over 8 million people listen regularly to

Agriculture is the backbone of the economy. Most of the workers in it are women.

VOK. New transmitters are being built, so that by the end of 1983 70 percent of the population will be able to receive VOK. Television broadcasting began in 1962. There are about 79,000 television sets and some half a million people watch them, the majority in urban areas. Forty hours of television are broadcast every week, mainly in English and Swahili.

Females make up just over 50 percent of Kenya's population. The majority of the workers in agriculture, the backbone of our economy, are women. But the role our women are playing in the economic and social development of the country gets very little coverage in the media as a whole. Women are not considered newsworthy! Women are only talked about in relation to the family, the home, fashion and cooking. I've founded the Association of Media Women to try to alter the situation. If we can make women who work in the media understand the importance of their sex to the Kenyan nation, then, perhaps, they can communicate it through the radio, television, newspapers and magazines. People, both men *and* women, should be more aware of the vital role that women are playing in our development.

"Christianity has played an important role"

The Reverend George Wanjau, 50, has been the Minister of St. Andrews Church, in Nairobi, since 1973. Married, with four sons, he lives in Milimani, a quiet suburb of the capital city.

Kenya is a very religious country. There is complete freedom of worship, so nearly all religious groups are represented. Nairobi, like all other big cities in Kenya, is dotted with churches, cathedrals, mosques and Hindu and Sikh temples.

Christian missionaries first came here in 1844. They settled on the coast and then began extending inland through Ukambani and Kikuyu to the Rift Valley, Nyanza and western regions. Now there are some twenty-five Protestant Churches and missions at work in various areas of Kenya, and about fifteen Roman Catholic societies. Christianity has played an important role in the development of this country. The first missionaries taught people to read and write, to farm, and trained people in such crafts as carpentry and masonry, and also in health care. So you can say that the foundations of

A tall, decorated tree dominates a park in Nairobi at Christmas-time.

modern Kenya were laid by the Church, and its work is continuing today.

The European missionaries who came in the nineteenth century were followed by many Indians. A lot of them were skilled craftsmen who helped to build the Kenya–Uganda railroad; others helped to start Kenya's industry. Asians still play an important part in our commercial world and are now part of Kenyan society, as are their religions.

Islam, too, has had an influence on our development. Islam came to Kenya at the turn of the seventh century with traders from the Persian Gulf. The Arabs set up city-states in Lamu, Malindi, Kalifi, Pate, Shanga and Mombasa. The Muslims had control of the coastal region twice: from 700 to 1550, and from 1730 to 1890; between these periods it was in the hands of the Portuguese. Because Islam started at the coast, there is naturally a larger concentration of Muslims, mosques and Islamic schools there than in other parts of the country, although Islam has spread all around Kenya.

People often wonder what I do during the week. They think that I only work on Sundays! During the week, people come to me with all sorts of problems which I try to help them solve. Also, I meet couples who are planning to get married. I talk to them about married life and how they are going to care for one another and make the best use of resources God will give them, emphasizing their relationship with God, which is very important.

Man's relationship with God is set out in the Scriptures. Our catechism teaches that Man's chief aim is to glorify God: to live a life that is pleasing to God in our homes, in our places of work, and in society at large; to make sure that we reflect the love of God which He has put in our hearts and in our everyday life.

Pope John Paul II preaching in a Nairobi cathedral during his visit to Kenya.

"Education is not yet compulsory"

Elphas Nyerere Olato attends a private secondary school in Nairobi. He lives with his father in a one-bedroom government apartment in Embakasi, just outside Nairobi. His mother and her seven other children live on their farm in the Western Province.

The education system in Kenya is based loosely on the British one. We have seven years of elementary education (Standards 1 to 7), followed by six years of secondary education (Forms I to VI). I've read that in 1981 there were some 4,134,300 children in elementary schools and about 464,700 in secondary schools. Education is being given priority by the government. It is not yet compulsory, but the government

hopes that by the middle of the 1980s everyone will receive a basic education. At the moment, 30 percent of the national budget is devoted to basic and higher education. In 1981/82, the Ministries of Basic and Higher Education spent K£164 million, K£107 million of which was on elementary education.

I go to a coeducational private secondary school in Nairobi. I went to elementary school in my home town, Kakamega, but my father is a civil servant in Nairobi and he asked me to come here for my secondary schooling. I wanted to go to one of the government-aided schools, but they were all full by the time I got here. There are more than 2,000 secondary schools in Kenya. Most are supported by the government, but a few are privately run. The standard of education in aided schools is generally better because they have to adhere

Women buying bananas in the main street of Kakamega, Elphas's home town in the Western Province.

strictly to the rules laid down by the government, and a student is provided with a school uniform and some books. Private schools are usually run as profit-making organizations, which has resulted in a lowering of their standards. Although they have to fulfil certain requirements laid down by the government, they seem to be able to get away with a lot. You have to buy your own uniform and books at private schools.

I'm in Form III. At the end of grade school, I had to take the CPE (the Certificate of Primary Education). I have one more year before I take exams for my East African Certificate of Education (the equivalent to O levels in Britain). If I pass in Grade 1, I can continue up to Form VI and then take exams for my East African Advanced Certificate of Education (the equivalent of A levels in Britain). Passing makes me eligible for the university. Pupils who don't want to complete their secondary education, but want to go to a technical college to learn a trade, can take the KJSE (Kenya Junior Secondary Examination).

During my vacations – in April, August and December – I go back to our *shamba* (farm) near Kakamega, where we grow corn. Kakamega is both the name of a town and of a district in the Western Province. The Western Province is populated by the Luyia people. There are some 2,119,700 of them, and they are the second largest ethnic group in the country. Almost half of them live in Kakamega, and it has one of the highest population densities in Kenya – nearly 700 people per square kilometer (1,800 per square mile), compared with the national average of 27 (70 per square mile).

Kakamega is in savanna country, and has a good rainfall during the first half of the year, and almost nothing during the

Morning assembly at the elementary school in Kakamega that Elphas went to before he came to Nairobi.

second half. Corn, cotton, coffee, sugarcane and some tea are the main crops of the area. I've been told that there was a short-lived gold rush there in the 1930s.

For visitors who like walking or jogging, there is a network of footpaths around Kakamega where it is common to meet the Luyias enjoying their music, dancing or playing soccer. Luyias like to relax by dancing and playing music and they are one of the few peoples in Kenya to use masks in their dances. They use a number of instruments for their music, including flutes, two-stringed fiddles, and horns.

23

"There are nearly 3,000 Kisii carvers"

Kennedy Kaunda Ombasa is a soapstone carver in the family business. He was named after President Kaunda of Zambia and President Kennedy of the U.S. Kennedy lives with his parents and seven brothers in Tabaka, a village in Kisii District, in Nyanza Province.

Our people, the Kisii, have been carving soapstone for some time. It's our medium of expression. People are always writing or saying flattering things about our art, which makes us very proud. There are many famous Kisii carvers. They're an inspiration to the people, like me, who are following in their footsteps. One of the most famous carvers is Elkana Ong'esa. One of his huge pieces is now in front of the Unesco (United Nations Educational, Scientific, and Cultural Organization) headquarters in Paris.

As a child of 4, I used to play with the chips from my father's carvings. Gradually, I began carving small things, like fishes and eggs. My father helped me until I could carve medium-sized pieces, like a small cup or a bird. Then I learned how to make animals, like elephants and hippos. Now that I've been taught the skill of carving, I don't want another job. I work about seven hours a day and get enough money from selling my pieces both locally and in the cities and towns.

The soapstone comes in various colors – white, black and pink. Pink is the most popular. It's dug in the Tabaka Hills. We get our stone from a quarry about 10 kilometers (6 miles) away. We bring it here on our heads. We use a *panga* (a large knife) to break it into the sizes we want. Then we cut these roughly into the shape of the object we want to carve. Using a *Kisu* (a small knife) we carve the stone. When it's finished, we wash it, then polish it with sandpaper and, finally, clean it with a brush. We usually make animals, fish and birds; skilled carvers also make human figures, and highly skilled people, like Ong'esa, make abstract pieces.

Not only do we make our own pieces from scratch, but we also buy unfinished pieces from local carvers. They're usually of poor quality, so we improve on what's been done, polish them to give them a better finish and then sell them. When we've gathered a reasonable stock together, from our own carvings and those we've bought, we pack it all into some boxes and carry them down to the bus stop. There we can get a bus or *matatu* to Nairobi or Mombasa. We sell our carvings to tourist shops there and to the African Heritage shop in Nairobi, which has a large selection of African handicrafts.

Soapstone carving is the basis of the Kisii economy. There are nearly 3,000 Kisii carvers. No other tribes carve soapstone, although a few of the Wakamba people are starting to. The industry has expanded a lot in the past decade. It's good that more people have got jobs, but it has also increased the competition, which has led to a lowering of the individual carver's income. Those who can make a lot of carvings can earn about 20 shillings a day from selling them. Small carvings sell for about 2 to 4 shillings, and take about fifteen minutes to make. A big piece can sell for 50 shillings, and takes about two or three days to make. Tourists normally have to pay double these prices when they buy the

Kennedy and his family in front of the small hut in which the children sleep.

pieces in the stores. Soapstone carvings are sold all over the country, mainly to tourists. They like to buy large animal pieces to take home.

Soapstone being sawed up in the quarry in the Tabaka Hills near Kennedy's home.

"Kenya is famous for its good tea"

Jackson Tarus, 28, is a tea-picker on a small farm in Kaptel, north of the town o Kapsabet, in Nandi District. He is single and lives in a room in the workers' quarters on the farm.

Kenya is famous for its good tea. Its flavor is popular with tea drinkers in Europe, North America and the Middle East. Most of Kenya's tea is grown in twelve districts, stretching from Kitale to Meru. There is also a tea belt running about 160 kilometers (100 miles) along the eastern slope of the Aberdares, from Limuru to Nyeri.

The big plantations are found to the east o the Rift Valley and on the western slopes of the Mau Escarpment.

A lot of tea is grown around Kericho. That's where the large plantation companies are located. Kericho, Sotik and Nandi are the oldest tea-growing areas. In Kericho there's the old Tea Hotel, which serves what must be the freshest tea in the world! The tea estates (plantations) around the town are delightful to see: vast fields of shiny-leaved, green bushes growing in neat rows.

Tea-picking goes on throughout the year. It's amusing to see the rows of tea-pickers on the estates with their bright-yellow, plastic aprons. They carry baskets on their backs. We pick "two-and-a-bud." That's two leaves of the tender shoot of a tea plant. I get paid 150 shillings a month, about a third of what I could get working as a laborer in the town.

Tea-pickers are paid according to the amount of tea they have picked during the day.

The tea-growing areas lie at an altitude of between 1,800 and 2,400 meters (6 to 8,000 feet). Kericho, known as "the most fertile tea area in the world," has an ideal climate for tea growing. It gets plenty of rain for most of the year. There are also hailstorms occasionally, which harm the tea buds and leaves. It can also get very cold. So it has an ideal climate for drinking tea as well!

There are about 138,000 small-sized tea "farms" in Kenya, each averaging less than a hectare. Together they grow 36 percent of Kenya's tea. In all, they cover 53,586 hectares (133,965 acres), producing about 146,000 tons of green tea leaf, or about 33,000 tons of ready-made tea. Small plantations, with mature tea bushes, earned on average K£217 per plot in 1982.

Tea-pickers on an estate near Kericho, one of the oldest tea-growing areas in Kenya.

Kenya has many tea factories. Two more are being built. A factory, such as the one in Nyeri, is supplied by about 3,400 growers. The factories are about 11 kilometers (7 miles) apart. Leaf-collecting centers are located between them. Tea farmers don't have to carry their crop for more than two kilometers (1.5 miles).

Kenya, as a whole, has some 56,000 hectares (140,000 acres) of planted tea. The factories aim to produce about 21.6 million kilos (47.5 million lb) of tea each year. Tea is priced at about 18 shillings per kilo (8 shillings a lb). Last year producers earned K£80.6 million. Just over 82,000 tons of tea is exported annually.

"We're trying to conserve our wildlife"

Sam Ng'ethe is Park Warden of Nairobi National Park, in charge of Kenya's Animal Orphanage. He comes from the Kiambu area, north-west of Nairobi. Married with four children, he lives in a three-bedroom prefabricated house in the grounds of the Park.

In Kenya, we're trying to conserve our wildlife, particularly those species that are in danger of becoming extinct. But that's only half the job really, because if you are protecting a species, you've also got to preserve its natural habitat – its "home." We've set up our National Parks and Game Reserves to do both of these tasks – to conserve our animals *and* their environment.

Kenya has about 40 conservation areas. These are made up of 17 National Parks, 2 State-run National Reserves, and the remainder are Game Reserves and Forest Reserves. Tsavo, where I used to work, is the largest National Park, extending for some 20,800 square kilometers (8,000 square miles) between Nairobi and Mombasa. The Nairobi National Park, where I now work, covers 113 square kilometers (44 square miles). It's about 8 kilometers (5 miles) from our capital. All our conservation areas are under the control of the Wildlife Conservation and Management Department. It has been estimated that 5 percent of Kenya has been set aside for wildlife conservation.

The animals in this park were not brought here. They've always been here. They move about freely. We only protect

Sam playing with "Kambe," a baby cheetah with an injured front paw.

them. More have moved into the park because of the protection they get. Part of the park is fenced because it is close to the residential areas of Nairobi. On the southern side, the River Athi forms a natural boundary, where animals come in and go out freely. In the dry season, from November, or during a drought, many animals from the neighboring Kajiado District come into the park: herds of wildebeeste, zebras and elands. Other animals found here are cheetahs, lions and even rhinos, buffaloes and ostriches.

The animals come into the park when it's dry outside because, apart from the permanent river, we've made small dams in suitable areas within the park. So when there is not enough grazing land outside, they know instinctively that there is plenty to feed on in the park. When the rains come, they know that there will be new grass growing on all the plains outside, and plenty of water to drink. Then they disperse and begin to move away.

The animal orphanage is for injured and sick wildlife or abandoned baby animals. There are now nearly 300 animals in the orphanage, which is spread out over 10 hectares (25 acres). It's open to visitors, but we don't display animals, as they do in zoos. They're here because they need our help.

If we get a young animal, we raise it until it can look after itself. Then it's released into the wild.

If an animal cannot go back to its natural surroundings, it is kept here permanently. But we try to help an animal readapt to the wild. As you know, the rule of the jungle is survival of the fittest. Once an animal is weak and unable to look after itself, it becomes an easy prey to a lion or cheetah. This means that an animal which has been injured or maimed during an attack by another animal, or fallen into a trap or snare, has to be rescued by our rangers on patrol, because it will need help and care.

We used to have a lot of problems with poachers. They hunted animals in remote areas for food or commercial reasons – elephant tusks, rhino horns, and zebra and lion skins could be sold for a lot of money. Now the Wildlife Department's anti-poaching campaign has improved the situation considerably. Game hunting has been banned and so has the sale of animal skins and ivory. Now the wildlife population is thriving.

Parts of Nairobi National Park border on the suburbs of the capital city.

"The demand for money is very high"

Mildred Owuor is the first woman to be employed as a manager with the National Bank of Kenya, which is owned by the government. Born and bred in Regea, near Kisumu, in Nyanza Province, she has a degree from Nairobi University.

Kenya has a fairly advanced financial system for a developing nation. Banking plays an important role in our economy. At the moment, the demand for money is very high. There just isn't enough to go around: the less you have, the higher the demand. Our financial system is dominated by fifteen commercial banks. They have about 300 branches around the country. Four of these banks are Kenyan and the rest are foreign. Until recently, the majority of the foreign banks were European or Asian. The 1970s saw an influx of American banks, and the early 1980s have seen the arrival of Arabian banks. In addition, we have about two dozen non-banking financial organizations, such as housing finance companies, installment plan firms and insurance companies.

The National Bank of Kenya is an ordinary commercial bank, but it is owned by the government. The bank was set up in 1968 and now has branches in Mombasa, Eldoret, Nakuru and Kisumu, as well as four in Nairobi. We cater mainly to the *wananchi* (the ordinary citizen) who doesn't have large projects to finance.

Mildred with her husband and two young sons outside her home in Nairobi.

Most of the private and foreign banks are only interested in the large firms in Kenya: one big loan to a firm and they can live off the interest payments for the rest of the year!

Banking is a very important career, very relevant for the country now. I joined the National Bank of Kenya in 1974, right out of Nairobi University, where I got a degree in commerce. I was the first female manager hired by the bank. Looking back, I suspect I was a guinea pig in an experiment to see how a woman would cope with the world of banking. But I'm now in a senior position, as are about half a dozen other women. More Kenyan women are now involved in business. Women used to be frightened even to walk into a bank. Women are sometimes still frowned upon for earning an income, but things are changing. It's now quite acceptable for a woman to borrow money from a bank to start a business. Those who have tried and succeeded have encouraged others. So, many men are now allowing their wives to run their businesses.

The Central Bank is the main institution in our financial system, being the government's bank. It also advises the government on its monetary policy, that is, controlling the amount of money flowing into and round the economy. The Central Bank controls the operations of the commercial banks, informing them of the sectors of the economy which the government wants to expand and which it wants to contract, so that the banks can lend more money to the former and less to the latter.

The direction in which our economy grows is determined by the government's Development Plan. Each plan forecasts the development of the country, both socially and economically, during the next five years. The current plan was drawn up in

The head office of the National Bank of Kenya in Nairobi, where Mildred works.

1979 and will last until 1983. During this period, the government planned to spend K£2,749 million, K£991 million of which was for expanding the economy.

"One of my poems has 217 verses"

Ahmed Sheikh Nabhany has been a renowed Swahili poet since the age of 12. He was born on Lamu Island, which he visits regularly. He works as a clerk in the District Commissioner's office in Mombasa, where he lives with his wife and two sons.

On Lamu, there has been a long tradition of poets. They have inherited the talent from their ancestors, but only a few are gifted; fortunately I'm one of them. I've worked hard at it; even so, I still write things which surprise me. I feel as if I couldn't have written them.

My ancestors were poets. On my mother's side, my grandmother, *Bi* (Lady) Amina Abubakr Sheikh, was a well-known poetess; she was like a "queen" of poetry. She began training me to be a poet when I was 12. I had always heard her reciting poems or singing songs, and I became interested in following in her footsteps. Her mother, *Bi* Khadijah Binti Abubakr, was a poetess; so was her sister, *Bi* Kupona.

When I first started writing, my grandmother looked at what I did and realized that I could become a poet. On Lamu, it's customary for those who don't know how to write poetry to go to those who know, to have poems written for them. When people had visitors or a wedding and they

This Lamu craftsman is making model dhows to sell to tourists visiting the island.

A Lamu dhow builder working on the wooden hull of a medium-sized dhow.

needed some poems to recite, they would ask my grandmother to write something for them. Our poems are also recited at funerals and at the birth of a child.

Often, when my grandmother had too much work, she would let me help out. That was how I started and developed, until I was able to survive on my own.

Swahili is very important to us. We still have many *wananchi* (citizens) who cannot read or write. They rely on the spoken Swahili, which helps in preserving the oral culture. It is the national language of Kenya and is taught in schools. We have radio and television programs in it, and even our Members of Parliament have to know basic Swahili to be elected.

Our poems deal with various themes: the history of a place; praising our heroes; giving advice; encouraging our fighters; or strengthening our faith. My poetry tries to capture the traditional ways of my people – the Swahili way of life. One of my poems is called *"Sambo wa Kiwandeo"* or *"Dhow of Lamu,"* which has 217 verses. For as long as I can remember, dhow building has been a way of life for some of our people.

We used to have a different kind of dhow here, called a *mtepe*, held together with ropes, no nails. But look around you. There are none left. They've all vanished! You will only find them in stories. So, I felt that even the dhow you see today, the *jahazi* or *sambo*, might disappear. Our children may never know what skills their forefathers had and how well they used them. My poem explains how dhows are built.

Poetry is not difficult for me now because, whenever the words come, I jot them down. Every now and then I find I have to write. When I don't, I feel I'm missing something.

"Indian culture has had an impact on Africans"

Jayantilal Ramji Chheda is a 50-year-old Indian businessman. His family firm, along with many others, is on Biashara Street in Nairobi. *Biashara* is Swahili for "business." He lives with his family in a five-bedroom bungalow in Parklands, a quiet suburb of Nairobi.

We Asians are a people who can live in any part of the world. Wherever we live, we try to improve the conditions in the country. We have tried to build up Kenya. Asians have played an important role in the development of Kenya's industry. We began by opening small stores. Slowly these developed into big stores, and factories to supply them began to be built.

There's a good future for industry in Kenya. Since Kenya became independen in December 1963, business has pro gressed considerably because people have worked hard on *shambas* (plantations) t produce a coffee boom, although the cur rent recession all around the world ha affected things.

I came to Kenya in 1950. My wife wa born here. She went to India for the firs time a couple of years ago. The 78,60(Asians, Hindus and Muslims living here are now in the third generation.

We are a family business. It was started about sixty years ago by an uncle, along with some other relatives. We are one o the largest wholesalers of textiles. We also specialize in furniture and carpets. Ninety percent of our business is wholesale, tha is selling goods to other tradesmen.

It is a competitive field. You have to know what you are doing, because you don't select your designs, quality, and

Jayantilal relaxing at home with his wife and two daughters.

colors properly, then you cannot sell anything. We're now very experienced. We've learned a lot from our forefathers. We work very long hours, and are careful about how we spend the money we earn.

Asian businessmen have helped their fellow African businessmen a lot. If you go outside Nairobi, you'll find that African traders are doing very well. We assist them with credit facilities. I have a lot of African customers to whom I give goods on credit for three to four months.

We also help them with our commercial know-how. Because we've been in this trade for a long time, we know what goods sell well. So, the people I sell the goods to know that they can trust me; they won't be let down and have a pile of articles that no one wants to buy from them.

Our African rivals have made good progress in business. Now, there are a lot of businesses which are run jointly by Africans and Asians. In fact, most of the firms in Kenya are in the hands of Africans. They even have monopolies in certain areas. They are now in an advantageous position, which is right: after all Kenya is their homeland.

We enjoy living here because we have a good standard of living – as do most other Asians. There is political stability and the economy is in good shape. We still have faith in Kenya and its leadership. We are Hindus, but we have freedom of worship.

There is racial harmony here. Many things are common to both Indian and African cultures, such as the importance of your family and a belief in God. A lot of Africans now take part in Hare Krishna, Hare Rama religious and cultural festivals. The Indian culture has had an impact on Africans.

We have brought up our children here, educated them both here and abroad, and married them here, according to our culture, which is important because, we believe, once culture is gone, everything is gone. So, we have been able to preserve our social structure intact. We don't miss India. It's a nice life for us here. We are lucky to have settled here. We are grateful to this country.

Biashara (meaning business) Street, Nairobi, where Jayantilal's shop is situated.

"Kenyans are now living longer"

Dr. Eric Mngola is a highly qualified consultant with a private practice in Nairobi. He's not sure of his age; all he knows is that he was born on a Sunday. Born and bred in the Taita Hills, near Mount Kilimanjaro, he is married with four children.

Our medical services have improved a great deal in recent years. In 1981, we had 221 hospitals, 262 health centers and some 1,100 pharmacists. We had 177 hospital beds for every 100,000 pharmacists. In the same year, there were 2,254 doctors and dentists, or 14 per 100,000 people, and some 600 doctors and dentists were being trained. Three-quarters of all doctors work in the private sector and not for the government, although most of them do some work for the government, as I do. Although I have a private practice, I run a special clinic once a week at the Kenyatta National Hospital, here in Nairobi.

Medical treatment is free, and most people live near a hospital. Each of the eight provinces has a general hospital and there are smaller ones in the forty-one districts into which the country is divided. In addition, there are many clinics and health centers in towns and villages. Unfortunately, there are long waiting lines in government-run hospitals. Those people who can afford to be treated privately are fortunate in being able to avoid waiting for treatment. Aside from the lines, most people seem content with our medical services.

Many more Kenyans are now coming to hospitals and health centers for treatment. In days gone by, many of them preferred to go to their local herbalist or witch doctor before coming to a doctor. They are no longer suspicious of modern medicine. Kenyans are now living longer: the average life span of a Kenyan is between forty and sixty years.

Communicable diseases still take up a lot of our time. Common diseases in Kenya, and indeed in the whole of Africa, are malaria, gastrointestinal diseases, diarrhea, sleeping sickness and hook worm. We are now beginning to take more notice of the diseases that are common in more advanced countries, such as diabetes, coronary heart diseases, and rheumatoid arthritis. Ten years ago, these illnesses were not regarded as common in Kenya. It's not that they weren't here then,

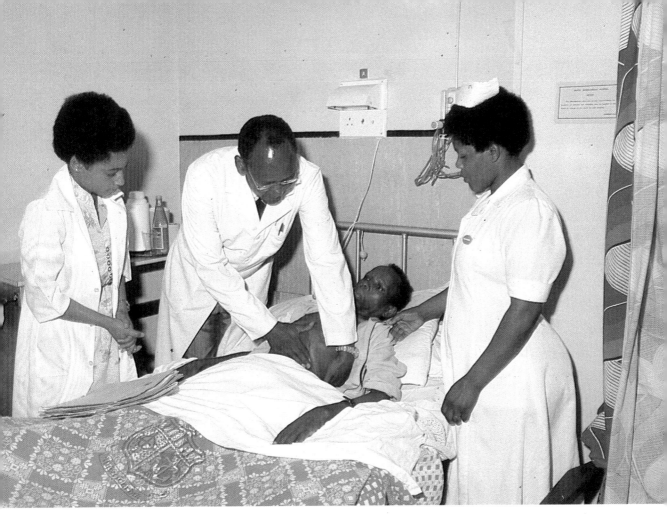

but that we weren't aware of them. With our improved medical facilities, we've been able to detect them and discovered them to be quite common. In another ten years, they'll probably be as important in public health as the illnesses we've always been treating.

My main hobbies are farming and gardening. I own a small farm in the Taita Hills, near Mount Kilimanjaro, where I was born and bred. I try to go there on the weekend. The Taita Hills are primarily an agricultural region. Millet, corn, cassava, sugarcane, bananas and beans are grown there. Because rich grazing land is limited in this area, animals used to take second place to the growing of crops, but the situation is changing. Much of the meat for the Taita people used to be obtained from

Dr. Mngola examining a sick patient in his clinic in Nairobi.

hunting, but the creation of the Tsavo National Park – the biggest in Kenya – in the plains restricted hunting to the hills, and the game there was gradually wiped out. Now more and more Taita people are acquiring cattle.

A view of the Taita Hills where Dr. Mngola has a small farm which he visits at weekends.

"Curios tell you a lot about our people and life"

Timothy Mutinda Ngao, 33, sells curios from his street stall in Nairobi, the city where he rents an apartment. His wife and four children live in his hometown of Kitui, and he visits them every other month when he buys his new stock of curios from the Wakamba tribe.

My curios are very popular with tourists. They like to take souvenirs back with them to remind them of their visit to Kenya. Most of my curios are only for decoration around the home, but some have a practical value, like the woven baskets I sell which can be used for carrying groceries. The most popular things I sell are the carvings of animals, such as elephants, rhinos and leopards. Most of these are carved out of wood by the Wakamba tribe.

The Wakamba (there are about one and three-quarter million in the tribe) live mainly in the Eastern Province. This area often suffers from drought, so the people have turned to non-agricultural trades. They once carved ivory, which is now forbidden, and made things out of metal, such as brass anklets. I buy my stock of wood carvings direct from the tribe, usually every other month.

Most tourists are surprised to learn that my curios are made by hand. They think that they've been made by machine because the finish on them is so good. Most of the curios that I sell can also be bought in stores, but tourists seem to prefer to buy them from kiosks like mine, which are on most streets in our towns and cities. It's probably because they're about 50 percent cheaper than those in the stores. On top of this, it's customary to bargain over prices at street stalls. You can't do that in the stores and supermarkets!

My customers also get better service

It's cheaper to buy curios from a street kiosk than from the shops, because you can bargain.

A famous Kenyan wood-carver at work in front of his home with his wife and child.

than they would in a store. Most of the storekeepers are not natives of Kenya, so they don't know anything about the lives of tribes like the Wakamba, the Wakikuyu or the Masai, but I do. Curios tell you a lot about our people and life in Kenya. I can tell people about the history behind a curio, why it was carved and how it was made, so that they can learn a little about our past.

There's a skill in selling curios. To begin with, you've got to have customers. I advertise myself verbally, attracting the attention of passing tourists and persuading them to come over to my stall before they go into a store. You also have to know about the types of wood which are used for carvings. Some of the woods are of poor quality and get spoiled by the sun. Because I know about these woods, I can tell my customers how to prevent this happening – by putting oil on them or dyeing them. Few storekeepers know about this and, what's more, don't seem to care about

what they sell. They just want the money. I think that's wrong because we're part of the tourist industry and we should take care and pride in "selling" Kenya to foreigners. But I'm not saying that the money is not important. Selling curios is my livelihood. On a very good day, I can earn K£200.

Tourism is an important industry in Kenya and it has expanded rapidly since the mid-1960s. Most of our tourists come from Europe – especially Britain and West Germany – and North America. I've read that in 1965 there were only 3,000 hotel beds in Nairobi; now there are 15,000. Down on the coast, things have developed even more, from just under 1,000 beds to nearly 10,000. I've also been told that we earn at least K£60 million a year from tourism. It's nice to know I am contributing, even in a small way to this.

"Everyone is free to worship in their own way"

Sheikh Ramadhan Gathiyaka Ghathaika, 65, is the *imam* of the Jamia Mosque, a historic building in the center of Nairobi. Approximately 6 percent of the population of Kenya is Muslim.

In Islam, an *imam* is the person who leads the congregation of worshippers in the five daily prayers (or *salat*) at a mosque. An *imam* also has to help in the development of Islam. He has to deal with and speak on Islamic matters. He has to teach those who follow him in the ways of Islam gently, not forcefully.

Above all, an *imam* has to be God-fearing, calm and well-versed in his religion. He has to study Islam and all its tenets in the Qur'an, the Holy Book, so that he knows the laws (or *sharias*) governing the religion. He has to observe the designated hours of prayers punctually: at dawn, in the afternoon, in the evening, at dusk and at night. He mustn't be away from the mosque at these times without a good reason.

I have a very responsible position in the Muslim community. Not just anyone can get up and go to the *mihrab* (the place at the front of the mosque where the *imam* stands to lead the daily prayers). An *imam* has to be someone who has studied the daily prayers fully.

I began reading the Qur'an at the age of 7, with the help of the late Sheikh Maalim Haji Umar. Then I studied Islam under another learned scholar, Sheikh Ali Bin Khalid, who came from Lamu Island. In 1943, I opened my own *madrassah* (an Islamic school), called Madrassah-tu-Saada, here in Nairobi.

My parents named me Ramadhan in honour of the holy month of Ramadhan in which I was born. Ramadhan is the month during which the Holy Qur'an descended to mankind through the Prophet Muhammad (may Allah's peace be upon him). During Ramadhan, all Muslims must fast each day between sunrise and sunset. Muslims are named after Islamic festivals, such as Rajab, Sha'aban and Idd. Some are named after the Prophet Muhammad himself and the other prophets, such as Ibrahim (Abraham), Musa (Moses), Issah (Jesus) and the Prophet Muhammad's companions, such as Abu Bakr.

This is the *Jumaa* (or Friday Mosque),

where Muslims come for their Friday prayers. It is managed by the Jamia Mosque Committee, which also runs a health center and an Islamic bookshop.

In Kenya, everyone is free to worship in their own way. We Kenyans as a whole – whether black, brown or white; or from the east of the country or the west – are one people. Our relations with other religions are good. The only difference between us is in the way we pray. People pray according to their beliefs, but in the development of Kenya, we unite as one people. We stand together in our prayers for the well-being of our country.

A lot of people – Muslims, non-Muslims, students and tourists – visit the mosque every day, and many come to talk to me. Some ask me religious questions; others ask me to pray for them. I pray to Allah to lighten their burden. When I do so, it's not because I'm a healer or that I have a big book in which I can look up the solutions to their problems. No. I only

The Jamia Mosque in Nairobi of which Sheikh Ghathaika is the imam.

pray to God because I know that He is the one who provides and He is the one who holds back. Allah is the creator of all the planets. Allah is the one who controls our lives.

The lost city of Shanga, one of the earliest Islamic settlements on Kenya's coast.

"In the past, women weren't educated"

Lucy Njeri Kenyanjui is a 24-year-old student at Nairobi University. She is studying commerce and plans to work for a market research firm after graduating. She and her four brothers and two sisters were raised in Kiambu, where their parents still live.

Nairobi University is very young. It started in 1956 as a technical college, largely to train people in engineering and business. After Independence in 1963, it became part of the University of East Africa along with the colleges in Makere, Uganda, and in Dar-es-Salaam, Tanzania. It became a full-fledged university in 1970, the only university in Kenya. Kenyatta University College, outside the city, is also part of it. There are just over 5,000 students on the main campus and just over 2,000 at Kenyatta College. Another university is now being planned.

I've always been interested in commerce, so I decided to study it at the university. I'm in my third year now and will graduate at the end of next year, when I would like to join a market research firm, helping to find out how firms' products are selling. The university now offers a wide range of degrees in the social sciences, the natural sciences and the arts. About 60 percent of the teaching staff are foreigners.

There are many female students in our faculties. About 32 percent of the 1981/82 incoming university students were female. Students from other countries made up 3 percent. Only a few girls used to

The modern campus of Nairobi University where Lucy is studying for her degree in commerce.

study commerce because it was regarded as a boy's subject. This year there are nearly 200 people studying it, about a quarter of whom are female.

In the past, women weren't educated. Girls were expected to stay at home and help out until they got married. But now we can go to school and climb up the educational ladder and then take up a career. Most educated women now want to have a career before they get married so that they are not totally dependent on males. We want more independence now.

People in Kenya used to look upon the university as the pinnacle of our education system. The "educated" person used to be respected. But things have changed recently because a person with a degree is no longer a novelty and because many graduates have "dropped out." University riots have also alienated the public from us. Being a successful businessman now seems more important than being an educated person. Consequently, many undergraduates are very disillusioned. The government has just set up a committee to investigate the running of the university, with the aim of making it more relevant to the needs of a developing country.

My brother is at a university in India. Over 9,000 Kenyans are studying abroad, 3,000 in India alone. They're either sponsored by our government or the government of the country where they're studying, or paying for the courses themselves.

Graduation day at the university. Lucy wants to work for a market research firm after graduating.

"The fishing industry in Kenya is booming"

Alex Obudha, 32, is a fisherman. He lives in the small fishing village of Dunga, near Kisumu, right on the shores of Lake Victoria in Nyanza Province. He lives in a one-room, thatched house with his wife and son.

I've been fishing since I was 12, and I'll probably continue being a fisherman for the rest of my life, just like my father, who taught me the trade.

The cheapest and traditional way of fishing in these parts is known as *ngogo*. The fish are caught in traps, like bell-shaped baskets, made out of papyrus and reeds. We catch *tilapia* and *ngege* in these traps. *Ngege* is a popular fish throughout Kenya. Catching fish with traps is mostly for beginners, though.

Most of my fishing is done with long lines. To catch Nile perch, I use a line with about 400 hooks. Nile Perch (or *puta* in Swahili) is common in East Africa, and delicious to eat. It's a large species which can weigh up to 100 kilos (220 lb). Each line costs 450 shillings, and the floats on them 10 shillings each.

Some of the fishermen around here only use nets. Sardines (*dagaa*), which are almost as popular as *ngege*, are caught with gill nets, which resemble mosquito nets. These nets are now made in Kisumu by a Japanese firm, but they are expensive, costing over 1,000 shillings each. Seine nets are also used. These are much bigger than gill nets and more expensive – about 7,000 shillings each. Since you need five or six of these nets, only the wealthy fishermen can afford to catch fish with them. Seine nets are taken out into the lake in a boat and dropped in a circle. Then two gangs of men haul them into the shore, trapping any fish in the way.

In Dunga, we have a fishing cooperative of about seventy fishermen, which I belong to. All the members of the cooperative bring their catch to Dunga, where we sell it for between 1.50 and 2.50 shillings per kilo, depending on the size of the catch. Some of the fishermen from nearby villages also bring their catch here, so we often have some 2,000 kilos (4,400 lb) of fish for sale. The fish are either sold whole or cut up into chunks and slices with *pangas* (large, sharp knives).

Fishsellers buy the cooperative's fish and then sell it in the towns and cities;

whole *tilapia* and fillets of perch, for example, are taken from here to Nairobi in refrigerated trucks. Local tradesmen also buy our fish to sell in the village markets around here. Some of the *tilapia* and *dagaa* are dried in the sun before being sold; a small proportion are smoked.

The fishing industry in Kenya is booming. In 1981, I've been told that 63,785 tons of fish were caught, with a value of K£7.3 million – 63 percent higher than the value of the previous year's total catch. Fish from Lake Victoria alone made up about 68 percent of the 1981 catch – 43,374 tons. Lake Victoria is Kenya's largest freshwater source of fish, followed by Lake Turkana and Lake Baringo.

Down on the coast, big game fishing is a growing sport. You can catch swordfish, barracuda, marlin, shark and bonito. Lamu, Kilifi, Malindi, Watamu and Shimoni are the main centers. If you go diving on the reefs along the coast, you can catch starfish, octopus, crabs, and prawns.

Lake Victoria, shown above, is Kenya's largest freshwater source of fish.

Fishermen from Dunga lay their nets out after another day's fishing on the lake.

"Some tourists want their own lion!"

Charles Kimani Kariuki, 36, is a safari guide who drives tourists around Kenya's national parks and game reserves. He has been doing the job for about ten years. He receives about a dozen letters or postcards every week from tourists he has shown around.

I have to be very knowledgeable about Kenya because tourists are curious about everything: from stones and plants to the types of animals and the climate. Most people are no problem but some are very difficult to please. Some tourists want their own lion – one that no one else has seen or photographed! Finding one can be quite a problem.

Kenya is a miniature Africa. That's why it's so popular with tourists. Seeing Kenya, its peoples, its landscape, makes you feel you've seen other parts of Africa too. Kenya has a wide range of landscapes, from the seashores of the Indian Ocean on the east, to the snowcapped peaks of Mount Kenya to the north, and Mount Elgon to the west; from the slopes of Mount Kilimanjaro to the south, to the highlands of the Aberdare Mountains. There are thick forests in the Aberdare Mountains, and near-desert country in the northwest and northeast regions.

Aberdare National Park, some 766 square kilometers (295 square miles) in

On safari in a balloon: some tourists getting an uninterrupted view of Kenya's wildlife.

area, is in the Aberdare Mountain range. The famous Treetops and The Ark lodges are in the park. From them you can observe wildlife either during the day or by floodlight at night. The Aberdares have a temperate climate: misty mornings, and bright days. Among the animals found in the Aberdares are lions, magnificent antelopes, elephants and rhinos.

Amboseli National Park is popular with tourists because it reaches to the slopes of Mount Kilimanjaro. Much of it is flat, so safari vans and buses can leave the roads and drive close to the animals. You cannot do this in most parks. But, while the tourists enjoy it, it disturbs the animals, who may be grazing peacefully or concentrating on a kill.

The Masai Mara Game Reserve has been described as "the Queen of Kenya's faunal sanctuaries." It forms part of the great Serengeti ecosystem on the Tanzanian border. It is savanna country where elephants roam. Because of its rich grazing land, there are an estimated one million wildebeeste and many Thomson gazelles.

Few tourists leave Kenya without catching sight of Mt. Kenya, 5,117 meters (17,058 feet) high.

The Marsabit National Reserve is in a desert region of Kenya, 690 kilometers (430 miles) from Nairobi, on the way to Addis Ababa. An elephant, named Ahmed of Marsabit, used to roam around the reserve. Because of his fabulous tusks, which reached the ground, he was protected by a presidential decree, providing him with a twenty-four hour guard of game wardens. He died naturally in 1974. An exact replica of Ahmed now stands in the National Museum in Nairobi.

The Marsabit District is inhabited by the Gabra, Rendille and Borana desert tribes. They are pastoral tribes, following their camels and cattle around as they seek grazing pastures. The Rendilles used to practice infanticide on the "second son or subsequent sons delivered on a moonless Wednesday." They considered it ill-fated to let them live. It's a hard life for these tribes; they often have to dig wells for themselves and their livestock.

47

"In the past we didn't sell our cows"

Abdullah Wako Boru, 42, is a Borana herdsman, who comes from Sololo, near Moyale, in the Eastern Province. He has about 20 head of cattle and 50 goats which provide him with an income and food. He is married, with four children.

Our lives may have changed, but a Borana will always be a herdsman in spirit. We keep cattle and goats. I have about 20 head of cattle, and about 50 goats. They're kept in a *boma* (an enclosure made out of dried thorn branches). We live in mud huts, thatched with grass to keep them cool. It can get very hot up here. January is the hottest month, with temperatures of 30°C (86°F). We're up before 6 a.m. We check the *boma* every morning to see that the livestock are safe. Our livestock are often taken by human thieves and wild animals.

If a wild animal, such as a lion or a cheetah, attacks cattle, you're bound to hear. Then you come out with a spear and scare it away. Wild animals get scared easily if you shout or throw something at them. But it's much more difficult if they've made a kill. Then they want to defend it. However, a cattle thief is much quieter, and you're lucky if you hear him. He quickly catches one of your animals and then runs away into the night.

If you're up early, and discover a cattle thief has robbed you, you can track his footprints in the sand. If you find him, you can be sure there will be a fight! If he defeats you, well, you lose your cows. If you win, then you retrieve your livestock. You can be killed. We used to have a lot of problems with *shiftas* (cattle rustlers). They used to raid *bomas* with guns, spears, and bows and arrows. But the government went after them and stamped them out.

We milk the cows before the sun rises. We keep the milk for ourselves. Those who live near towns sell their milk to the townsfolk. Milk is important to us. It's all we used to have for a whole day. We didn't bother about other food. Nowadays we eat *ugali* (a thick gruel made from corn flour and water). Meat? Oh yes! We eat meat, but again not as much as we used to.

Sometimes we slaughter a goat. Some of the meat is roasted on an open fire; the rest dried in the sun.

After milking, we take the herd out

to graze. When there's no grass around, they have to make do with what they can find. At midday, we take the herd to drink water. Our water comes from a well. We have to scoop it out, either with a *debe* or a skin bucket. Then the herd goes grazing again till the evening. We get back home by 6 or 7 p.m. After the herd is back in the *boma*, we rest a little, drink some milk, and then settle down to a meal.

In the past we didn't sell our cows. They were your wealth. What more did you want? Only recently have we begun to sell them. Now you can sell your cows at cattle markets and get between 1,000 and 1,500 shillings a head. Previously, you used to just sit and watch your herd grow. It could be big enough to require ten *bomas*. A rich Borana could have had between two and three thousand head of the best Borana stock. But selling and cattle rustlers have diminished our stock. Even I used to have a much larger herd.

A Borana woman uses a camel to carry things to another village.

Hungry Borana cattle find some greenery in the arid landscape near Marsabit.

"During Ramadhan we serve special food"

Omar Adam Yusuf, 36, owns a restaurant, called Malindi Dishes, on the outskirts of Nairobi. He specializes in Swahili dishes from Kenya's coastal region. He is married and has three children.

My restaurant is unique. It's run both as a business and as a place where people can meet for a chat. I am a Swahili from the coast, so I specialize in the Swahili foods from that region. These are mostly foods which are cooked in a rich coconut-milk sauce. They are both salty and sweet. Some of the common ingredients in Swahili dishes are cassava, bananas, beans, and peas.

We make a number of snacks from rice, wheat, and gram (bean) flours. Common snacks are *mkate wa sinia*, a sort of rice cake; *mahamri* or *mandazi*, sweet, doughnut-like pastries, made from wheat flour; and *Bhajias*, which are originally Indian, made from gram flour, but we also have distinctly Swahili ones made from dhal.

Swahili dishes and their ingredients come from a variety of cultures, including Chinese, Indonesian, Persian, Arabic, and Indian. They're a hodgepodge of all these cultures.

Our popular meat dishes are *mchuzi*, curry; *kababu*, kebabs; and *mishkakis*, barbecues, which include chicken. We have sea foods, again cooked in thick coconut sauce, like *samaki wa kupaka*, a whole fish; and vegetables such as *mchicha*, wild spinach; and desserts including *tango* and *boga*, pumpkins; *viazi vya maziwa*, sweet

Omar checks that his cook isn't burning the kebabs on the barbecue!

potatoes; *tambi ya papai*, strips of green pawpaw cooked in milk, coconut, and sugar; and *kaimati*, succulent balls of wheat dough, deep-fried in oil and soaked in syrup. These are some of the Swahili dishes liked by people.

We welcome our clients by offering them *kahawa*, black coffee, in tiny cups, which is an Arabic tradition. Foreigners and tourists come, off and on, to taste Swahili dishes, but we rely mostly on people who live in this area.

During the holy month of Ramadhan, we serve special foods, called *iftar*, meaning food for breaking the fast. We prepare more varieties than on ordinary days. During Ramadhan, we are closed during the day because, as Muslims, we cannot serve people with food when we ourselves are fasting. We open in the evening, before sunset, for the Muslims who are fasting.

Then we also provide a take-out service before the time to break our fast. The funny thing is that we get more non-Muslim take-out customers, who want to sample our special dishes, than Muslims themselves. They come to appreciate some of our Islamic customs during Ramadhan.

We're in a busy area. At peak hours, we get over 150 people, a little more than we can accommodate comfortably. Hotels and restaurants are important businesses in Kenya, because many tourists use them. Many use the restaurants in the center of Nairobi, which are expensive. Malindi Dishes is on the edge of the city, so we are a bit cheaper than them. An average meal here costs just under K£1.

A lot of people think that the restaurant trade is very profitable, but we only have 15 percent profit margin. I do enjoy my work because I like meeting people.

Omar often helps out in his restaurant, serving hungry customers with Swahili food.

"The drain of works of art out of Africa is worrying"

Joseph Murumbi, 71, is an art connoisseur and collector. A former Vice-President of Kenya, he has now retired from politics. He lives on his 800 hectare (2,000 acre) ranch in Nyanza Province. He owns a shop in Nairobi which sells and exhibits African art.

I've always been a collector. Even when I was young, I used to spend the little money I had on books or small works of art rather than on drink or other pleasures. I've lost my collection twice. As a student in England, I ran out of money and couldn't pay my rent, so my landlord took all my things. Then in 1941 I was away from Kenya for several years and when I got back, I found a friend had sold my entire collection!

I was a political exile in England when we were struggling for *Uhuru* (Independence or Freedom for Kenya). A number of

An election rally in Masai country, where Joseph has an 800-hectare (2,000-acre) ranch.

other Kenyan politicians were also there, including *Mzee* Jomo Kenyatta. He was one of the fathers of the Kenyan nation. He's called *Mzee* out of respect. He became the first President of Kenya after we won our *Uhuru* from British colonial rule in 1963. After Independence, I was appointed Minister of State, then Foreign Minister, and finally Vice-President.

I managed to rebuild my art collection when I was traveling abroad on government business. I gathered together a collection of works of art from virtually the whole of Africa, as well as from Europe, China, and the Orient. The African art means the most to me. We must do more to preserve our African heritage and encourage African artists to continue to produce material that reflects their cultures. I don't believe that our gifted young artists should be sent away to study at art schools in Europe or North America. Take a look at the carvings of the Makonde people. There's no one in any art school in the world who can teach an African sculptor how to carve this kind of work. It can only be learned in the villages where the Makonde sculptors live and work.

Foreign art schools and their teachers are important for the technical training they can provide, but they have their dangers, too. I've seen so many promising young African artists from England, Italy and North America who have lost their African roots. They produce good work, but it's no longer truly African in spirit. We need to set up art schools in Africa, with teachers who are non-academics from our towns and villages.

The drain of African works of art out of Africa is worrying. Many African countries now have laws preventing the export of their art works. My art collection has been bought by the Kenyan government,

Joseph has specialized in collecting art from all over the African continent.

so it will remain here. Recently, it was put on display and a lot of people came to see it. I'm now Chairman of the Archives Advisory Council which is helping the government set up a national art collection. My own works of art have laid the foundations for this project.

"There are about 20,000 matatus"

Joseph Rukwaro, 25, is a *matatu* driver. *Matatu* is the popular Swahili name for a minibus which picks up commuters on their way to and from work. Joseph lives in a one-bedroom apartment in Eastleigh, a suburb of Nairobi, with his wife, Charity, and their three children.

This is a difficult job. You can't simply walk into it. It takes a while getting used to. I used to work for an Asian who hired out *matatus*, charging a shilling a kilometer. In a day you could drive 250 or 300 kilometers. It was up to you to earn as much as you could.

I worked hard and saved as much as I could so that I was able to buy my own *matatu*. It carries twenty-two passengers. It's twelve years old, so it needs looking after.

I always try to get my passengers to work on time. I don't like it when people complain about being late. I'm very pleased when a passenger boards my *matatu* again, because I know then that I am providing a good service. I know most of my best customers by sight.

Some *matatu* drivers are reckless. They're not careful, and cause accidents. But, at least, these are usually not as serious as some of the pile-ups on our major highways. In 1980 we had 11,329 traffic accidents in Kenya, in which 2,228 people

lost their lives.

By the time I go to bed, I'm very tired. Driving this *matatu* all day exhausts me. Getting up in the morning becomes difficult. My whole body aches. But what can I do? I've got to earn money somehow.

There are more passengers commuting to and from Nairobi than our bus services can carry. We help carry the balance much faster.

We compete with buses on many routes, but some *matatus* cover routes not served by buses. The *matatu* got its name from the old fare of three ten-cent coins, called *mapeni matatu*. Now the fare is many times that amount.

Many people choose a *matatu* because they are in a hurry. If someone is late for work, we take him there much faster than buses. Unlike buses, *matatus* don't stop when they're full. A *matatu* can also take a shortcut, which a bus cannot.

There are about 300,000 vehicles on our roads, about 20,000 of which are *matatus*; some 3,000 of these are in Nairobi. We help move thousands of urban workers.

On a good day, I can carry up to 700 passengers. If I don't have a breakdown, I can earn 300 to 350 shillings a day, which is a good income. Those drivers with newer vehicles can do more trips than I can, and so earn more.

I start work before 7:00 a.m., and finish at about 10:00 p.m. When we're not busy, I rest for about an hour.

Sundays are easier. I stop at about 2:00 p.m. I do only a few runs to earn the following day's fuel, then spend the rest of the day with my family. The rise in gasoline prices has hit me. The buses haven't been hit so hard because they have diesel engines, and the cost of their fuel hasn't risen so much.

At times like this, matatu *drivers hope they have strong roof racks!*

(Above) Joseph picks up passengers in his matatu *on a street in Nairobi.*

"Many Kenyan girls are living on their own"

Amina Ahmed Jaberney, 18, is in her second year at the Kenya Polytechnic in Nairobi. She is training to become a medical secretary. There are only two polytechnics in Kenya; the second one is in Mombasa.

I've always attended girls-only schools. So I came here for a change, because it's co-educational. I'm enroled in a two-year course to be a medical secretary.

This is quite a new course. We're the third group in Kenya to take it. There are twenty-one of us in it. We were told before we started that we would be like "gold dust" when we finished, and that there would be no problems over getting a job. There are mostly girls in this course. I don't know why. It's probably because we've got nimbler fingers than men!

The polytechnic has many departments, including engineering, sciences, printing, institutional management, and commerce, which is the one I'm in. The secretarial course here is divided up into specialities, according to the type of job you want. There are courses for legal secretaries, medical secretaries, personal assistants, and audio-typists.

I think girls in Kenya should educate themselves – train themselves in areas where women don't usually work. In the engineering department, there are only seven girls. Technical courses are becoming increasingly important. Very soon, about half the courses in our secondary schools are going to be technical ones. So girls must start to widen their horizons.

Things are changing. Many Kenyan girls are now living on their own. But they're generally from well-off families, who can support their children. If your parents don't have much money, and especially if there are a lot of children, girls are expected to help out. This certainly applies to city people. I'm not too sure about the girls who come here from country villages. I think some of them do send money back home, while others forget all about their families.

My father is a businessman. I am the second child. My elder sister is a secretary, and my other sister and two brothers are still very young. So, when I start work, I'll have to help out.

I'll have to live with my family. They wouldn't agree to me living on my own. In

my community, it's not considered proper for a girl of my age to live alone. But I think it's wrong: a girl *can* look after herself. If you can reach your teens without getting into serious trouble, then you should be able to leave home. Let's face it, your parents are not with you in school, or in college. You have to look after yourself there. I think it's very wrong. Parents should give us more freedom.

I really like this polytechnic and the people here. It helps having people from

Kenya Polytechnic in Nairobi, one of two such institutions in the country.

different tribes in one place. It bridges the gaps between us. Everyone feels they're one. Actually, in the first term people used to keep to themselves – the Luos, the Asians, the Kikuyus. I'm the only Somali, but now we have got used to each other. We're all friends.

Students preparing for their afternoon classes during the lunch break.

Facts

Capital city: Nairobi (population about 1 million).

Principal language: Official language is Kiswahili (Anglicized to Swahili), derived from the Arabic *Sawāhila*, meaning coastal dwellers. About 75 different languages are spoken, including English, Kikuyu and Luo.

Currency: 100 cents=1 Kenya shilling; 20 Kenya shillings=1 Kenya pound (K£)=US$1.50 (Spring 1983).

Religion: No state religion. Most Africans follow their traditional beliefs, but the Christian influence is growing (at least 25% of the population). The Roman Catholic Church (1.5 million followers) has been developed by missionaries from Ireland, Britain, Holland and Italy. The Protestant Church was started mainly by British and American missionaries and now has some 950,000 followers. Muslims form 6% of the population. Islam has spread among some African coastal tribes and the cities. The Asians of the population are Hindus and Muslims, with the exception of the Goans, who are Roman Catholics. There is a great variety of religious beliefs and forms of worship between races and tribes, and between districts.

Population: 15,332,000 (1979). It is increasing annually at a rate of 3.8%. 50% of the population are under the age of 15; 74% are under 30. Kenya consists mainly of small towns of 3,000 to 10,000 inhabitants. The northern half of the country is sparsely populated. Most of the population are Africans. There are 126,000 Asians, 40,000 Europeans and 26,000 Arabs. Arabs and Swahilis are mainly on the coast. Inland are the races speaking Bantu languages, and non-Bantu tribes, such as the Luo, the Nandi, the Kipsigis, the Masai, the Somali and the Gallas. There are more than 40 tribes.

Climate: Varies with altitude. Land above 1,500 meters (5,000 feet) has a temperate climate with fairly good rainfall. Most of the north is dry. The coastal zone is hot and humid with a tropical climate.

Government: Kenya became an independent state and member of the British Commonwealth on December 12, 1963, after six months of self-government. On December 12, 1964, Kenya became a republic. The National Assembly, the Parliament, has one chamber with 172 members. 158 ar elected; the Attorney General and 12 members ar appointed by the President, the Speaker by th National Assembly; all members serve for fiv years. The President, currently Daniel arap Mo has executive power and is directly elected ever five years. Kenya is a one-party state. The countr is divided into the Nairobi area and 7 provinces.

Housing: This is a critical problem in Kenya. It is c poor quality in rural areas and in great demand i urban areas. Rural houses are mainly rectangula buildings made of mud, and thatched. Most house are rented.

Education: This is not compulsory and is predo minantly free. The Ministry of Basic Educatio deals with pre-school, elementary and special edu cation; the Ministry of Higher education with sec ondary, post-secondary and technical education After pre-school education, there is a three-tiered system: seven years of elementary education, fol lowed by four or six years of secondary education and then university or technical education. Th government is currently carrying out a program t eradicate adult illiteracy, and also to improve th quality of education in rural areas, especially in th arid north and northeastern parts of the countr where the population is primarily nomadic. Pupil are given free milk. There is a lack of qualifie teachers. Kenya has one university, the Nationa University of Nairobi. There are two polytechnics one in Nairobi and one in Mombasa, and about six teen technical colleges. Many university student study overseas, particularly in India.

Agriculture: This is the mainstay of the economy It provides 35% of the national income. About 79% of the working population is engaged in agricul ture. Tropical, sub-tropical and temperate crop are grown. Coffee, tea, sisal, pyrethrum, corn and wheat are important crops in the highland areas Coconuts, cashew nuts, cotton, sugar, sisal and corn are the main crops at lower altitudes. Only one-fifth of the total land area gets enough rain to sustain its agricultural production. Four-fifths o the land is used for grazing cattle and for wild game, a major tourist attraction. The main areas o crop production are the Central, Rift Valley Western and Nyanza Provinces, and parts of the Eastern and Coastal Provinces. Livestock farming varies from traditional herding of the Masai tribes

Glossary

to pedigree stock-raising of beef and dairy cattle on highland farms. Much of the agricultural land was owned by Europeans, but it is now in the hands of Africans.

Industry: Nairobi is the main industrial center and the headquarters of many commercial organizations operating throughout East Africa. Its main industries are brewing, soft drinks, flour milling, pharmaceuticals, textiles and clothing, cigarette manufacturing, light engineering, fruit and meat canning, and coffee processing. Mombasa also has an expanding industrial base, and is the largest port on the eastern coast of Africa. The other main centers of industry are Eldoret, Nakuru and Thika. Since 1970, industrial machinery has accounted for about 50% of the total value of imports, while food, beverages and consumer goods have fallen from 20% to less than 15%. Unroasted coffee, tea, petroleum products, meat products, pyrethrum, sisal, hides and skins, and wattle extract are the main exports. A large part of Kenya's trade is with Britain: in 1980 it imported £105,443,000 from Britain and exported £259,103,000 to it. Tourism has been an important industry since the mid-1960s.

The Media: The government-owned radio station, the Voice of Kenya (VOK), operates three services: one in English, one in Swahili, and one in sixteen languages. Over eight million people listen regularly to the VOK. There are some 1,404,000 radio sets in the country. A television service was started in October 1962. It can now be seen on over 78,600 TV sets. It broadcasts in English and Swahili for 40 hours a week, 16 hours of which are "live" programs. Some of the programs are imported from the USA and Britain. There are five daily papers, three in English and two in Swahili, and five weekly papers, all in English except for *Coast Week*, which is in English, German and Swahili. A wide variety of trade, technical and sports magazines are also published, most of them monthly. The Press is independent and uncensored, although it is expected to support government policies. There are over 38 movie theaters in the country, mainly in towns and cities; rural areas are served by mobile movie vans. Most of the films are imported, although a local film industry is being set up.

Co-operative A group of workers in the same industry, fishermen for example, who pool their resources and then share the income that they make from selling their goods.

Ecosytem Abbreviation for ecological system; the study of a particular area to see how its animals and vegetation interact over a period of time.

Henna A reddish dye obtained from the henna shrub or tree which is used in industry and for conditioning and coloring hair.

Kerosene Another name for paraffin, especially in the USA.

Masonry The craft of a mason. A mason is a person skilled in building with stone.

Monopoly A situation in industry where one firm has complete control of the manufacture and supply of a product.

Pastoralist A landholder who raises sheep or cattle on a large scale.

Pyrethrum An insecticide prepared from the flowers of Chrysanthemums.

Qur'an (Koran) The sacred book of Islam, believed by Muslims to be the word of God dictated to Mohammed via the angel Gabriel.

Ramadhan A period of thirty days during the Muslim year during which strict fasting is observed from sunrise to sunset.

Savanna Open grasslands, usually scattered with bushes or trees.

Swahili The Anglicized form of Kiswahili, the principal language of Kenya. The word is derived from the Arabic *Sawāhila*, which means "coastal dwellers." Swahili is now used as both a noun, as in "the Swahilis," and as an adjective, as in "Swahili food."

Index